Grace
and Grant

WITHDRAWN

Kelly Doudna

Consulting Editor, Diane Craig, M.A./Reading Specialist

Published by ABDO Publishing Company, 4940 Viking Drive, Edina, Minnesota 55435.

Copyright © 2005 by Abdo Consulting Group, Inc. International copyrights reserved in all countries. No part of this book may be reproduced in any form without written permission from the publisher. SandCastle™ is a trademark and logo of ABDO Publishing Company.

Printed in the United States.

Credits
Edited by: Pam Price
Curriculum Coordinator: Nancy Tuminelly
Cover and Interior Design and Production: Mighty Media
Child Photography: Steven Wewerka, Wewerka Photography
Photo Credits: AbleStock, Eyewire Images

Library of Congress Cataloging-in-Publication Data

Doudna, Kelly, 1963-
    Grace and Grant / Kelly Doudna.
        p. cm. -- (First sounds)
    Includes index.
    ISBN 1-59679-160-8 (hardcover)
    ISBN 1-59679-161-6 (paperback)
        1. English language--Consonants--Juvenile literature. I. Title. II. Series.
    PE1159.D685 2005
    428.1'3--dc22
                                                                        2004058983

SandCastle™ books are created by a professional team of educators, reading specialists, and content developers around five essential components that include phonemic awareness, phonics, vocabulary, text comprehension, and fluency. All books are written, reviewed, and leveled for guided reading, early intervention reading, and Accelerated Reader® programs and designed for use in shared, guided, and independent reading and writing activities to support a balanced approach to literacy instruction.

Let Us Know

After reading the book, SandCastle would like you to tell us your stories about reading. What is your favorite page? Was there something hard that you needed help with? Share the ups and downs of learning to read. We want to hear from you! To get posted on the ABDO Publishing Company Web site, send us e-mail at:

sandcastle@abdopub.com

SandCastle Level: Beginning

gr

ABCDEFGH
IJKLMNOPQ
RSTUVWXYZ

abcdefgh
ijklmnopq
rstuvwxyz

Grace

Grant

green

grasshopper

grapes

grapefruit

grill

The grass is 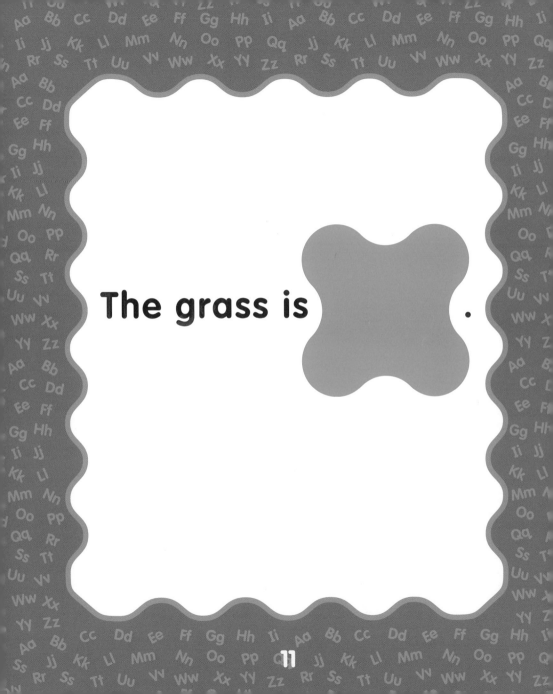 .

Here is the .

Here are the .

Here is the .

Here is the .

Grace has the grasshopper.

Grant has grapes.

The grasshopper
hops on the grapes.

Which of these pictures begin with gr?

More words that begin with gr

grandmother

grass

gray

great

grin

ground

group

grow

About SandCastle™

A professional team of educators, reading specialists, and content developers created the SandCastle™ series to support young readers as they develop reading skills and strategies and increase their general knowledge. The SandCastle™ series has four levels that correspond to early literacy development in young children. The levels are provided to help teachers and parents select the appropriate books for young readers.

Emerging Readers
(no flags)

Beginning Readers
(1 flag)

Transitional Readers
(2 flags)

Fluent Readers
(3 flags)

These levels are meant only as a guide. All levels are subject to change.

To see a complete list of SandCastle™ books and other nonfiction titles from ABDO Publishing Company, visit **www.abdopub.com** or contact us at: 4940 Viking Drive, Edina, Minnesota 55435 • 1-800-800-1312 • fax: 1-952-831-1632

31901060215920